Franz LISZT

HAMLET
Symphonic Poem No. 10
S. 104

Study Score
Partitur

PETRUCCI LIBRARY PRESS

INTRODUCTION

The present score is a reissue of one from the Franz Liszt-Stiftung edition, originally published by Breitkopf & Härtel from 1907-1936. The edition was prepared in an effort to publish the entire oeuvre of Franz Liszt. Editors included such prominent musicians as Béla Bartok, Ferruccio Busoni, Eugène d'Albert and José Vianna da Motta – some of whom studied with Liszt – as well as scholars like Peter Raabe, who would later compile the first catalog of the composer's works. The need for a complete edition was already apparent by the time of Liszt's death. Although some of his piano music had regularly appeared in new editions throughout his life, these works were by no means representative of even his pianistic output. A far more unfortunate fate was left for his orchestral music - which would usually be issued only once, soon to go out of print and later scarcely available. The Liszt-Stiftung edition revived many works that had fallen into relative obscurity and was therefore handsomely welcomed.

The edition was sadly never completed. The publication activity was brought to a premature end by the time of the Second World War. All in all the incomplete edition encompassed 34 volumes, among others two symphonies, the symphonic poems, some concert works, a couple of piano arrangements and 11 volumes of original works for piano – a mere fraction of the composer's output – but the edition would nonetheless break the ground for Liszt research during the 20th century for a number of reasons. First, it brought to light a number of late pieces that would put Liszt as a forerunner of experimental music and firmly establish his position as such. Second, it revealed the diversity of Liszt's output, which up until that time had been best known as an important addition to the piano repertoire. Third, it displayed the complex and characteristic nature of many of his works by being the first edition to show and make use of several alternative (sometimes vastly different) versions and sources. Last but not least, it would provide the world with a generally reliable edition of easy availability and very high standard for its day.

The Bavarian State Library acquired a complete copy of said edition and decided to digitize it in 2008. By that time more than 70 years had passed since its publication, effectively rendering the edition out of copyright and free for any use. Each and every page was scanned and uploaded to their online digital collection. While this was a great effort in itself, the site has a rudimentary interface, is difficult to navigate and the scores are not in the context of relevant information. One of our users decided to also upload it to our site, the International Music Score Library Project (IMSLP) / Petrucci Music Library, the unique wiki-based repository of musical scores, composers and indexes that anyone can edit and amend. Through the effort of a single user, Mattias K. (piupianissimo), the entire edition is now easily available worldwide to those who wish to perform and study the composer's music in a historical context, since as the case is with Liszt's music, many early editions exist and many are readily available on the site and many more will be available in the future. IMSLP is as such a valuable resource available to the scholar but even more to the performer who is always a mere mouse click away from scores that have not been in print since the turn of the past century, or that are otherwise hard to come by. The availability, quantity of ease of access for online scores will soon exceed those of the traditional medium of print. Nevertheless new works have always been published through the printed medium and this tradition is going to persist for many years to come even if complemented by the digital medium. Of course an important fact to stress is that the availability of digital scores online does not exclude the need of printed score since neither one can replace the comfort and neatness of one another. The quality of a bound reprint or new engraving exceeds that of a score printed at home.

I discovered IMSLP back in early 2006 when it first began. At that time many scores were scattered on the net either privately or on commercial collection sites. Many of these sites had a considerably large collection but sadly many had restrictions on number of downloads per day and the process of contributing to them was riddled with bureaucracy. IMSLP was the first free site where anyone could contribute and upload any kind of musical scores. I have personally searched and uploaded many works – particularly those of Liszt – and the future of the site is nothing but bright. At the time of its start only a handful of scores were available on the site but through the effort of its users IMSLP has grown to be the largest collection of scores available on the Internet.

Hamlet is the tenth work in a series of thirteen symphonic poems composed by Franz Liszt. It was composed in 1858 and first published in 1861 by Breitkopf und Härtel of Leipzig. The dedicatee is Princess Carolyne zu Sayn-Wittgenstein. This score is from the fifth volume of the Franz Liszt-Stiftung edition, edited by Otto Taubmann and published in 1909. The score, along with a number or arrangements, is also available directly at the following URL:
http:// imslp.org/wiki/Hamlet,_S.104_(Liszt,_Franz)

Soren Afshar (Funper)
Summer, 2011

COMPOSER'S PREFACE

Eine Aufführung, welche den Intentionen des Komponisten entsprechen und ihnen Klang, Farbe, Rhythmus und Leben verleihen soll, wird bei meinen Orchester-Werken am zweckmässigsten und mit dem geringsten Zeitverlust durch geteilte Vor-Proben gefördert werden. Demzufolge erlaube ich mir, die HH. Dirigenten, welche meine symphonischen Dichtungen aufzuführen beabsichtigen, zu ersuchen, der General-Probe Separat-Proben mit dem Streich-Quartett, andere mit Blas- und Schlag-Instrumenten vorangehen zu lassen.

Gleichzeitig sei mir gestattet zu bemerken, dass ich das mechanische, taktmässige, zerschnittene Auf- und Abspielen, wie es an manchen Orten noch üblich ist, möglichst beseitigt wünsche, und nur den periodischen Vortrag, mit dem Hervortreten der besonderen Accente und der Abrundung der melodischen und rhythmischen Nuanzierung, als sachgemäss anerkennen kann. In der geistigen Auffassung des Dirigenten liegt der Lebensnerv einer symphonischen Produktion, vorausgesetzt, dass im Orchester die geziemenden Mittel zu deren Verwirklichung sich vorfinden; andernfalls möchte es ratsamer erscheinen, sich nicht mit Werken zu befassen, welche keineswegs eine Alltags-Popularität beanspruchen.

Obschon ich bemüht war, durch genaue Anzeichnungen meine Intentionen zu verdeutlichen, so verhehle ich doch nicht, dass Manches, ja sogar das Wesentlichste, sich nicht zu Papier bringen lässt, und nur durch das künstlerische Vermögen, durch sympathisch schwungvolles Reproduzieren, sowohl des Dirigenten als der Aufführenden, zur durchgreifenden Wirkung gelangen kann. Dem Wohlwollen meiner Kunstgenossen sei es daher überlassen, das Meiste und Vorzüglichste an meinen Werken zu vollbringen.

Weimar, März 1856.

Pour obtenir un résultat d'exécution correspondant aux intentions de mes œuvres orchestrales, et leur donner le coloris, le rhythme, l'accent et la vie qu'elles réclament, il sera utile d'en préparer la répétition générale par des répétitions partielles des instruments à cordes, à vent, en cuivre, et à percussion. Par cette méthode de la division du travail on épargnera du temps en facilitant aux exécutants l'intelligence de l'ouvrage. Je me permets en conséquence de prier MM. les chefs d'orchestre qui seraient disposés à faire exécuter l'un de ces Poèmes symphoniques, de vouloir bien prendre le soin de faire précéder les répétitions générales, des répétitions préalables indiquées ci-dessus.

En même temps j'observerai que la mesure dans les œuvres de ce genre demande à être maniée avec plus de mesure, de souplesse, et d'intelligence des effets de coloris, de rhythme, et d'expression qu'il n'est encore d'usage dans beaucoup d'orchestres. Il ne suffit pas qu'une composition soit régulièrement bâtonnée et machinalement exécutée avec plus ou moins de correction pour que l'auteur ait à se louer de cette façon de propagation de son œuvre, et puisse y reconnaître une fidèle interprétation de sa pensée. Le nerf vital d'une belle exécution symphonique gît principalement dans la compréhension de l'œuvre reproduite, que le chef d'orchestre doit surtout posséder et communiquer, dans la manière de partager et d'accentuer les périodes, d'accuser les contrastes tout en ménageant les transitions de veiller tantôt à établir l'équilibre entre les divers instruments, tantôt à les faire ressortir soit isolément soit par groupes, car à tel moment il convient d'entonner ou de marquer simplement les notes, mais à d'autres il s'agit de phraser, de chanter, et même de déclamer. C'est au chef qu'il appartient d'indiquer à chacun des membres de l'orchestre la signification du rôle qu'il a à remplir.

Je me suis attaché à rendre mes intentions par rapport aux nuances, à l'accélération et au retard des mouvements, etc. aussi sensibles que possible par un emploi détaillé des signes et des expressions usitées; néanmoins ce serait une illusion de croire qu'on puisse fixer sur le papier ce qui fait la beauté et le caractère de l'exécution. Le talent et l'inspiration des artistes dirigeants et exécutants en ont seuls le secret, et la part de sympathie que ceux-ci voudront bien accorder à mes œuvres, seront pour elles le meilleur gage de succès.

Weimar, Mars 1856.

In order to secure a performance of my orchestral works which accords with their intentions, and which imparts to them the colour, rhythm, accent and life that they require, it is recommended that the general rehearsal should be preceded by separate rehearsals of the Strings, Wind, Brass, and instruments of percussion. By this division of labour time will be saved, and the executants will more rapidly be made familiar with what is required of them. I therefore venture to request that conductors, who are pleased to bring one or the other of my symphonic poems to a hearing will adopt the plan formulated above.

At the same time I may be allowed to remark that it is my wish that the mechanical, bar by bar, up and down beating of time, which obtains in so many places, should as far as possible be discarded, and that only the periodic divisions, with the prominence of certain accentuation and the rounding off of melodic and rhythmical nuances should alone be regarded as indispensable. The vitality of a symphonic performance depends upon the intellectual perception of the conductor, presuming that suitable material for its realisation is to be found in the orchestra; failing this it would seem to be advisable to hold aloof from works which do not claim a promise of every-day popularity.

Although I have endeavoured to make my intentions clear by providing exact marks of expression, I cannot conceal from myself that much, and that perhaps the most important, cannot be set forth on paper, but can only be successfully brought to light by the artistic capability and the sympathetic and enthusiastic reproduction by both conductor and executants. It may therefore be left to my colleagues in art to do the most and best that they can for my works.

Weimar, March 1856.

F. Liszt.

After the 1854 relief by Ernst Rietschel

INSTRUMENTATION

2 Flutes
Piccolo
2 Oboes
2 Clarinets
2 Bassoons

4 Horns
2 Trumpets
3 Trombones
Tuba

Timpani

Violins I
Violins II
Violas
Violoncellos
Basses

Duration: ca. 10 minutes

First Performance: July 2, 1876
Sonderhausen: Orchestra
Max Erdmannsdorfer, conductor

ISBN: 978-1-60874-030-7

This score is an unabridged reprint of the score
first issued in Leipzig by Breitkopf & Härtel, 1909. Plate F.L. 10

Printed in the USA
First Printing: December, 2011

HAMLET

Symphonic Poem No. 10

S. 104

FRANZ LISZT (1811–1886)

PETRUCCI LIBRARY PRESS

7

Fast dasselbe Tempo, aber allmählich beschleuni-
Quasi lo stesso tempo, ma poco a poco più animato

gend bis zu dem Buchstaben E.
sin alla lettera E.

Der Buchstabe R____ bedeutet ein geringes Ritardando, so zu sagen: ein leises crescendo des Rhythmus.
The letter R____ signifies a slight Ritardando, so to speak: a gentle crescendo of the rhythm.
La lettre R____ signifie un petit Ritardando, c'est-à-dire: un doux crescendo du rhythme.

*) Die Tremolos in den Bässen sehr dicht und schaurig.
The tremolos in the basses very dense and in a sepulchral manner.
Il faut que les trémolos des basses soient très fournis et horribles.

*) NB. Die beiden Achtel in dieser Figur überall sehr kurz abzustossen.
The two quavers in this figure to be played very short everywhere.
Dans cette figure les deux croches partout très staccato.

12

40307

16

18

20

22

23

*) NB. Dieser Zwischensatz, 3/2 Takt, soll äusserst ruhig gehalten sein und wie ein Schattenbild erklingen, auf Ophelia hindeutend.
This intermediate episode (3/2 time) must pass over like a shadow and be played in the most tranquil manner. It relates to Ophelia.
Cette phrase intercalée, 3/2 temps, doit être jouée d'une façon extrêmement paisible et doit donner l'idée d'une ombre désignant Ophelia.

26

27

30

32

34

38

O Vom Buchstaben **O** bis zum Buchstaben **Q** immer drängender.
Dalla lettera O sin alla lettera Q sempre più stringendo.

O Vom Buchstaben **O** bis zum Buchstaben **Q** immer drängender.
Dalla lettera O sin alla lettera Q sempre più stringendo.

40

41

42

44

R **Sehr langsam und düster. (wie Anfangs.)**
Molto lento e lugubre. (come primo.)

R **Sehr langsam und düster. (wie Anfangs.)**
Molto lento e lugubre. (come primo.)

46

50

BAND 5

HUNGARIA.
Symphonische Dichtung Nr. 9.

Vorlage: 1. Die erste Partiturausgabe, erschienen 1857 bei Breitkopf & Härtel in Leipzig. Verlagsnummer 9383.

2. Die autographe Partitur im Liszt-Museum in Weimar.

3. Kürzungen, zusammen mit dem Anhang zu den Festklängen 1861 erschienen. Verlagsnummer 10176.

Bemerkungen: Im 2. Takt hat die gedruckte Vorlage vom letzten Achtel im 1. Fagott zum 1. Achtel des nächsten Taktes einen Bogen, dessen Bedeutung durch den Staccatopunkt über der ersten der beiden Noten aber illusorisch gemacht wird. Der Bogen wurde daher, als vermutlich auf einem Versehen beruhend, gestrichen.

S. 12. Im 2. Takt der II. Violinen fehlt in der gedruckten Vorlage die Angabe *pizz.*, im 4. Takt die Angabe *arco*. Beide Hinzufügungen erscheinen als selbstverständlich.

S. 13, 5. Takt. Die verschiedenen Stärkegrade in den Klarinetten (*mf*) und Fagotten (*p*) für den Vortrag der gleichen Stelle sind von Liszt deutlich hineinkorrigiert worden.

S. 25 weicht in den I. Violinen der Anfang des Motivs [notation] von dessen sonstigen Fassungen, die so [notation] lauten, ab. Die Stichabschrift hat jedoch deutlich nur dieses Mal punktierten Rhythmus. Die Originalskizze hatte schon das erste Mal [notation]. Das wurde aber ausradiert. Bei der zweiten (der hier in Betracht kommenden) Stelle sind ebenfalls Radierspuren, aber trotzdem sind Punkte und 32tel-Strich deutlich stehen geblieben.

S. 28, 3. Takt wurde der in der gedruckten Vorlage vorhandene Bogen vom Achtel zur Halben des nächsten Taktes im Engl. Horn als augenscheinlich fehlerhaft — er kommt in keinem andern Instrument vor — gestrichen.

S. 83, vom Buchstaben O an hat die gedruckte Vorlage in gr. Flöten und Hoboen über dem gehaltenen *g* der I. Instrumente noch je vier Takte zusammenfassende Phrasierungsbögen. Da diese sich augenscheinlich auf die II. Instrumente beziehen, wurden sie auch zu diesen gesetzt.

* * *

HAMLET.
Symphonische Dichtung Nr. 10.

Vorlage: 1. Die erste Partiturausgabe, erschienen 1861 bei Breitkopf & Härtel in Leipzig. Verlagsnummer 10153.

2. Die autographe Partitur im Liszt-Museum in Weimar.

Bemerkungen:

S. 32 steht in der gedruckten Vorlage vom dritten Viertel des 4. Taktes zur Halben des nächsten Taktes ein Bogen nur für das zweite Horn; dafür steht nur über dem 1. Horn ein Marcatozeichen (>). Die Stichkopie hatte [notation], den Bogen für das 2. Horn setzte Liszt hinzu, die Originalskizze hat [notation], aber ohne >. Nach der Analogie späterer Stellen dürfte [notation] richtig sein.

* * *

www.ingramcontent.com/pod-product-compliance
Lightning Source LLC
Chambersburg PA
CBHW081350040426
42450CB00015B/3374